TARSIERS

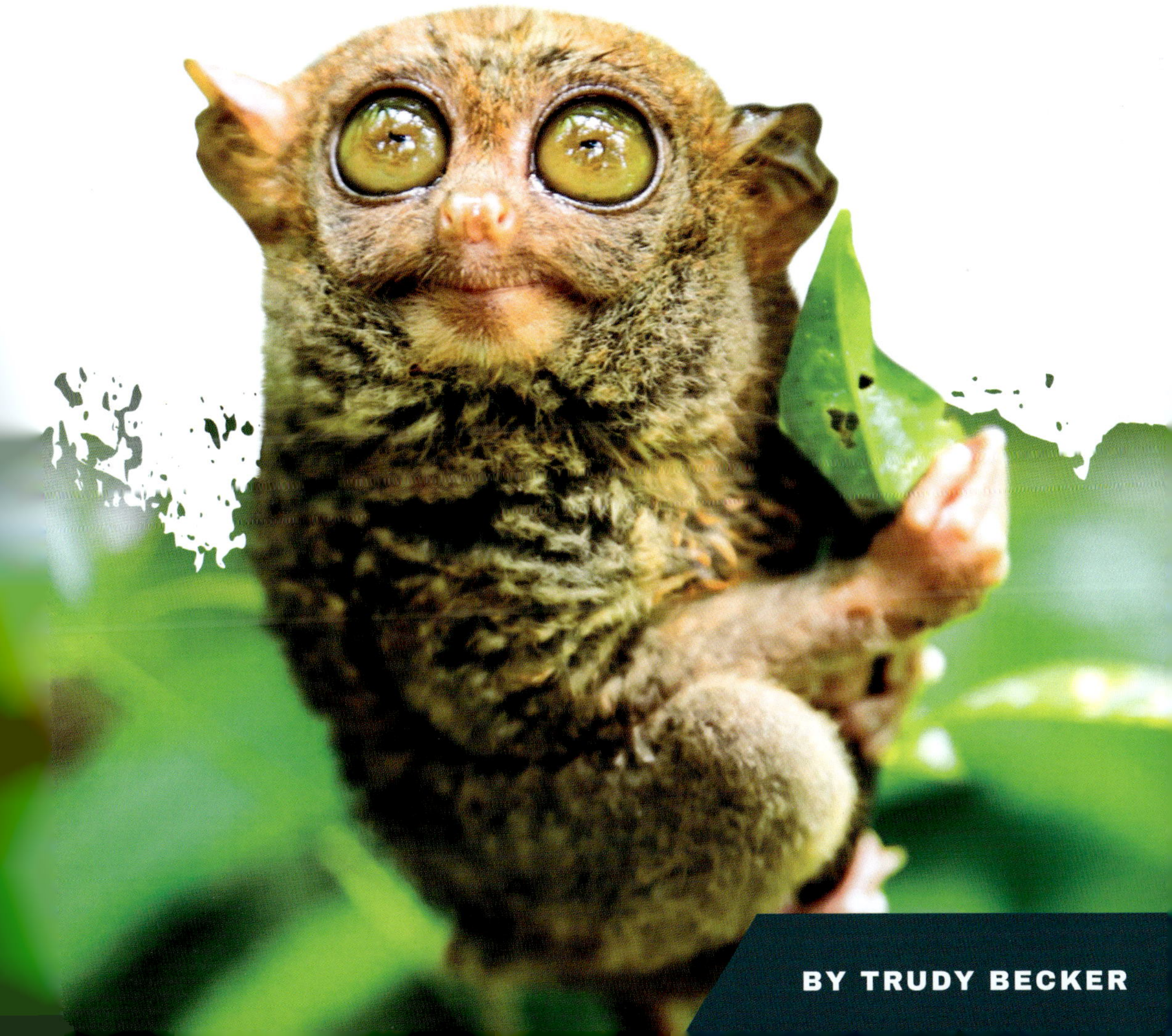

BY TRUDY BECKER

WWW.APEXEDITIONS.COM

Apex is distributed by North Star Editions:
sales@northstareditions.com | 888-417-0195

Produced for Apex by Red Line Editorial.

Photographs ©: Shutterstock Images, cover, 1, 4–5, 7, 8, 10–11, 14, 16–17, 18–19, 20, 21, 22–23, 25, 26–27, 29; Jurgen Freund/Nature Picture Library/Alamy, 9; iStockphoto, 12–13; Stuart Gray/Alamy, 24

Library of Congress Control Number: 2025939164

ISBN
979-8-89250-800-1 (hardcover)
979-8-89250-829-2 (paperback)
979-8-89250-885-8 (ebook pdf)
979-8-89250-858-2 (hosted ebook)

Printed in the United States of America
Mankato, MN
012026

NOTE TO PARENTS AND EDUCATORS

Apex books are designed to build literacy skills in striving readers. Exciting, high-interest content attracts and holds readers' attention. The text is carefully leveled to allow students to achieve success quickly. Additional features, such as bolded glossary words for difficult terms, help build comprehension.

TABLE OF CONTENTS

CHAPTER 1

FLYING TARSIER

A tarsier sits on a tree branch. The tiny **primate** is hungry. It spots a few beetles moving down on the forest floor.

Tarsiers eat about 10 percent of their body weight every day.

The tarsier leaps from the branch. It flies through the air. It catches the trunk of a nearby tree. Then it scurries down to the ground.

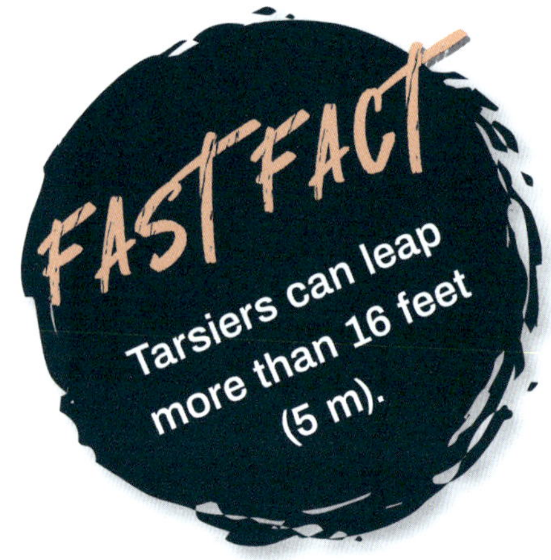

Tarsiers have sticky pads on their fingers that help them cling to things.

Tarsiers can grab flying bugs out of the air.

The tarsier pounces on a bug and eats it. Then the primate grabs a piece of wood. It pries more bugs out with a thin finger and eats them, too.

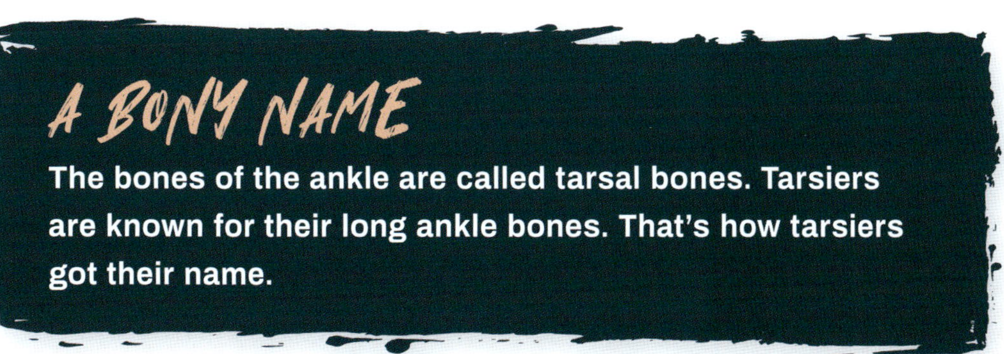

A BONY NAME

The bones of the ankle are called tarsal bones. Tarsiers are known for their long ankle bones. That's how tarsiers got their name.

A tarsier's long legs help it make big jumps.

CHAPTER 2

ALL ABOUT TARSIERS

There are at least 13 **species** of tarsiers. All tarsiers are small. Most are about the size of a tennis ball.

The Philippine tarsier is one of the smallest primates in the world. It weighs about 4 ounces (113 g).

Tarsiers have round bodies and big eyes. They have long, skinny fingers and toes, too. Their tails are twice as long as their bodies.

A tarsier's eyes are bigger than its brain.

Tarsiers live on islands in Southeast Asia. Most tarsiers live in rainforests or other areas with many plants. However, the number of tarsiers is dropping. People move into their **habitats** and cause problems.

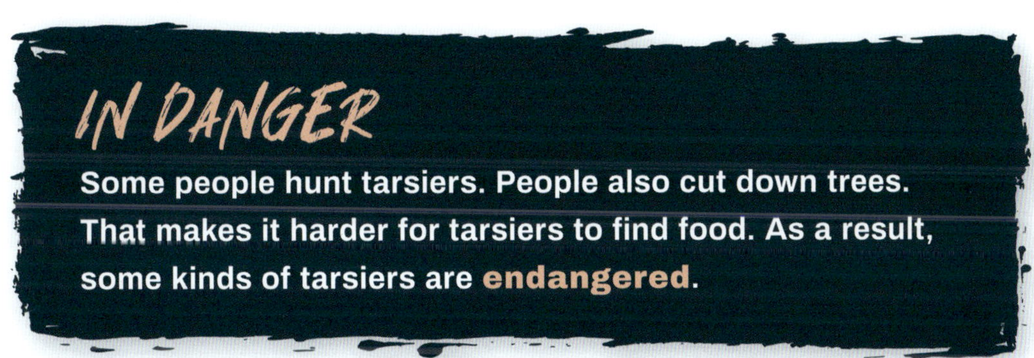

IN DANGER

Some people hunt tarsiers. People also cut down trees. That makes it harder for tarsiers to find food. As a result, some kinds of tarsiers are **endangered**.

◀ Western tarsiers live in parts of Indonesia.

CHAPTER 3

LIFE IN THE WILD

Tarsiers are **carnivores**. They mainly eat flying insects. But they may eat other small animals, too.

Tarsiers are the only primates that don't eat plants.

Tarsiers spend most of their lives in trees.

Tarsiers are nocturnal. At night, they search for food on or near the ground. When day comes, they climb up trees or hide in thick plants to sleep.

Tarsiers may make high-pitched sounds to tell other animals to stay away.

Some tarsier species live alone. Others live in pairs or small family groups. Tarsiers use high-pitched calls to **communicate** with one another.

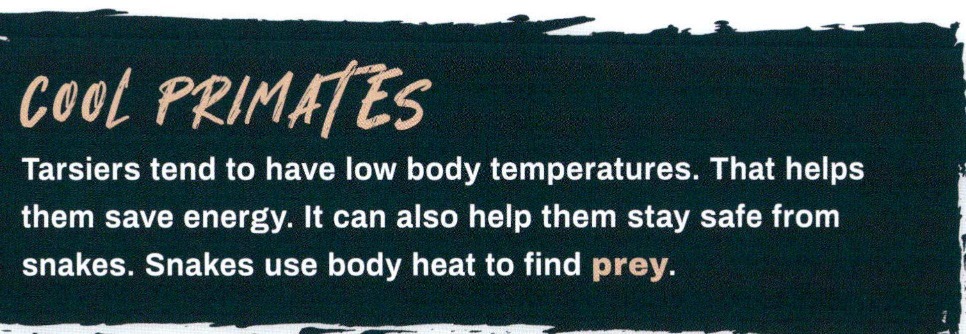

COOL PRIMATES

Tarsiers tend to have low body temperatures. That helps them save energy. It can also help them stay safe from snakes. Snakes use body heat to find **prey**.

Many animals hunt tarsiers. Monitor lizards are one kind.

CHAPTER 4

LIFE CYCLE

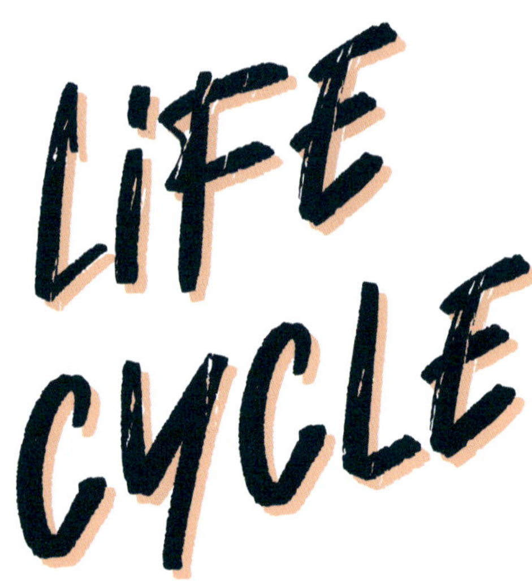

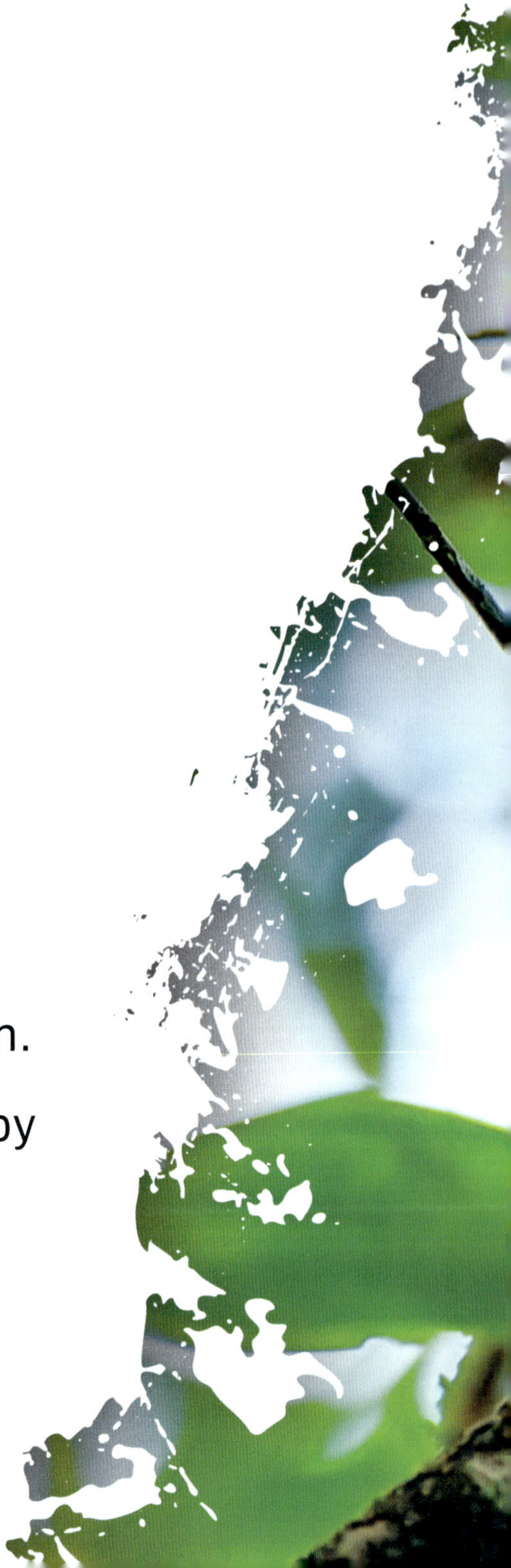

Tarsiers form close pairs and **mate**. About six months after mating, females give birth. Each female has one baby at a time.

Some tarsiers give birth twice a year.

Female tarsiers may carry their babies on their backs or in their mouths.

At first, babies stay close to their mothers. The mothers feed them milk. Within a few months, the babies can find food on their own.

LEARNING FROM MOM

Mother tarsiers teach their babies many skills. For example, mothers show their babies how to hunt. The babies watch and learn. Mothers also show them how to communicate.

Baby tarsiers can climb trees within a few days of being born.

A tarsier's home area can span a few acres.

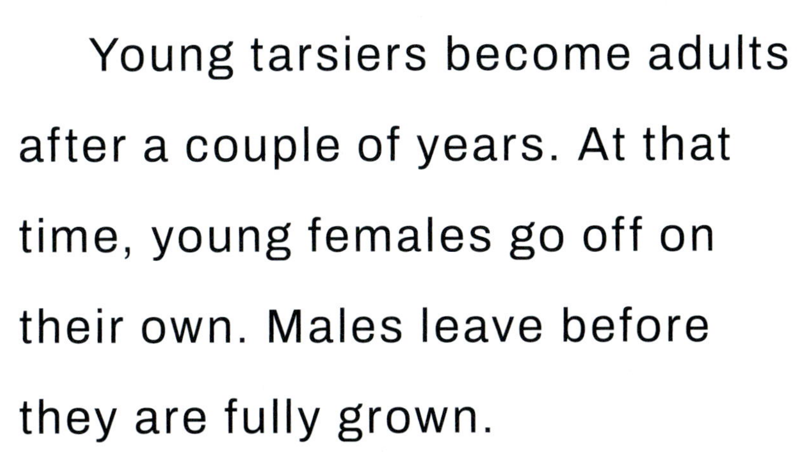

Young tarsiers become adults after a couple of years. At that time, young females go off on their own. Males leave before they are fully grown.

FAST FACT

Scientists don't know how long wild tarsiers live. **Captive** tarsiers have lived up to 16 years.

COMPREHENSION QUESTIONS

Write your answers on a separate piece of paper.

1. Write a few sentences about how tarsiers hunt.

2. Would you like to be awake at night like a tarsier? Why or why not?

3. How many babies does a female tarsier usually have at a time?

- **A.** one
- **B.** two
- **C.** six

4. How could low body temperatures help keep tarsiers safe from snakes?

- **A.** Tarsiers could move too slowly for snakes to see.
- **B.** Snakes could have a harder time finding tarsiers.
- **C.** Snakes could be too cold to catch tarsiers.

5. What does **pries** mean in this book?

*Then the primate grabs a piece of wood. It **pries** more bugs out with a thin finger and eats them, too.*

A. forcefully pulls
B. quietly sleeps
C. quickly climbs

6. What does **nocturnal** mean in this book?

*Tarsiers are **nocturnal**. At night, they search for food on or near the ground.*

A. awake and active during the day
B. awake and active at night
C. able to make their own food

Answer key on page 32.

GLOSSARY

captive

Kept by humans instead of living in the wild.

carnivores

Animals that eat meat.

communicate

To send and receive messages.

endangered

In danger of dying out forever.

habitats

The places where animals normally live.

mate

To form a pair and come together to have babies.

prey

Animals that are hunted and eaten by other animals.

primate

An animal in a group that includes apes and monkeys.

species

Groups of animals or plants that are similar and can breed with one another.

BOOKS

Becker, Trudy. *Aye-Ayes*. Apex Editions, 2025.

McCarthy, Cecilia Pinto. *Rain Forest Biomes*. Abdo Publishing, 2024.

Wilson, Libby. *Mind-Boggling Mammals*. Apex Editions, 2024.

ONLINE RESOURCES

Visit **www.apexeditions.com** to find links and resources related to this title.

ABOUT THE AUTHOR

Trudy Becker lives in Minneapolis, Minnesota. She likes exploring new places and loves anything involving books.

ANSWER KEY:
1. Answers will vary; 2. Answers will vary; 3. A; 4. B; 5. A; 6. B